In His Presence
There is Fullness of Joy
Volume 2

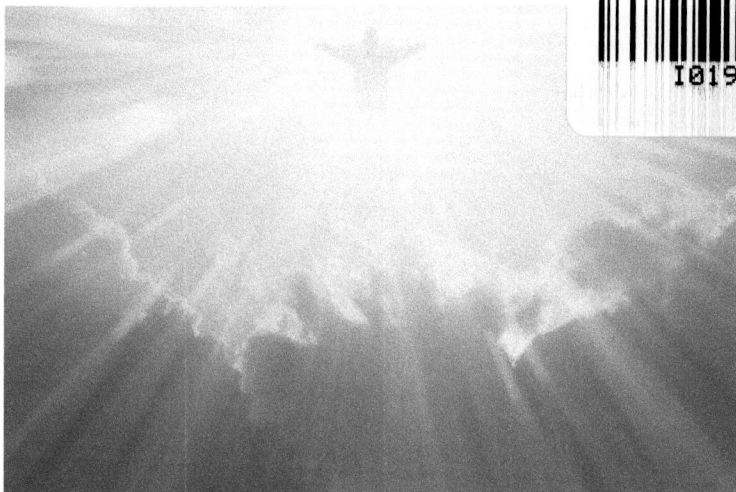

Presented to

By

Date

Joel 2:1

BLOW ye the trumpet in Zion, and

sound an alarm in my holy mountain:

let all the inhabitants of the land tremble:

for the day of the LORD cometh, for it is nigh

at hand;

In His Presence
There is Fullness of Joy
Volume 2

Pastor Dorothy St. Clair

Forsaking the Assembling by Paul O. Nichols

Originally published in ***The Christian Informer*** September 1997.

In HIS Presence: There is Fullness of Joy

Volume 2

Copyright 2018 by Pastor Dorothy St. Clair

First Edition, First Printing 2018

ISBN: 978-0-9968834-3-6

Pastor Dorothy St. Clair
P. O. Box 3953
St. Louis, MO 63136

Printed in United States of America
174 Chesterfield Industrial Boulevard
Chesterfield, MO 63005

Acknowledgements

Special thanks to God the Father, God the Son, and God the HOLY GHOST for looking beyond my faults and using me to spread the message of HIS SON Jesus Christ, for making it possible to tell of HIS Kingdom come on earth through book form, a vision given to me by GOD for HIS children. This book was born through faith and much pain but inspired by the HOLY GHOST.

I thank my husband Pastor Robert St. Clair who is my co-helper in the ministry/church, my daughter Demetria Strong (Meme), who thinks she is my mom she is so protective of us; my three grandsons who are the jewels of my life: Minister Christopher Strong, Desmond Strong, and Darrion Strong; and our daughter Rosiland who is in Heaven with Jesus

rooting and waiting for us. We love and miss you dearly.

Thank you all for being my family and believing in

me.

I thank the Word of Life Christian Church family

and our ministry staff:

Michelle Merriwether my photographer of volume 1

and volume 2 and son Michael Merriwether for

being watchmen for me when I work late nights.

And special thanks to Sister Stephanie Bess, my typist,

for being patient and ready to help in any way she could,

and she did. May God bless her forever. May God bless

you all in Jesus name.

"The Lord gave the word: great was the company of

those that published it" (Psalm 68:11 KJV).

Pastor Dorothy

Contents

Chapter 1: BEING IN THE WILL OF GOD

Let us pray: Father, we thank You for this opportunity to be in Your Presence. For Your Word says where two or three have gathered in Your Name, there You are in the midst.

"For where two or three are gathered together in my name, there am I in the midst of them" (Matthew 18:20 KJV).

So, we thank you for being in the midst today. Now, Father we ask that You open our eyes that we are able to see what You're showing us. Open our ears that we might hear what You're saying to us. Open our hearts, God, that we might receive the things that You are showing and telling us in Jesus name. Amen.

I feel like David when he said I was glad when they said unto me let us go unto the house of the Lord. I want to continue what I was doing in *In HIS Presence There is Fullness of Joy Volume 1*. Please feel free to get your Bible, and let's have Bible Study. We are going to go into another phase of it. We were talking about being in the presence of the Lord and the good things that are there-- in His presence. Hallelujah. That is where His Glory rests--in His presence. There may be some that do not know that there is something to gain by staying in the presence of God. Amen? Our main scriptures in *In HIS Presence There is Fullness of Joy Volume 1* comes from Psalms 16:11.

"Thou wilt shew me the path of life: in thy presence *is* fulness of joy; at thy right hand *there are* pleasures for evermore" (Psalms 16:11 KJV).

If you do not have Volume 1, and you want to put Volume 1 and Volume 2 together, you can go to our website: **stclamin.org** and purchase it or order it from Amazon.com (paperback and Kindle formats) and from other online bookstores in eBook format from Barnes and Noble NOOK, ebooks2go.net, overdrive.com, and others. You may also call 314-831-9525 and order it by phone.

David said: "Thou will not leave my soul in hell (in Sheol)." Thou will not leave my soul with the dead; neither will Thou suffer (or allow) Thy Holy One to see corruption.

"For thou wilt not leave my soul in hell; neither wilt thou suffer thine Holy One to see corruption" (Psalms 16:10 KJV).

Let us talk about this a little. What was David saying? He was saying there is a place in You God, where I can have peace of mind, where I am safe from all hurt, harm, or danger. David was saying regardless of what my troubles might be on this earth whether it is in my mind (soul) or in the physical realm of life--in my marriage, finances, it may be depression even oppression. If I would press into Your presence, get into Your Word, press into Your will, I shall be safe from all these woes of life and safe in Your presence. And there I will have fullness of joy in the midst of all my trials, which is the same as distress, sufferings, worries, anxieties and burdens.

Let us define the *Presence of God.* The word "presence" means "in the sight or company of someone, a place where a person is, something present." "Something (such as a spirit) felt or believed to be present" (Merriam Webster Dictionary online) "The state or fact of being present, the immediate proximity of a person or thing, and a divine or supernatural spirit felt to be present" (Free Dictionary online). **For God is a Spirit and they that worship Him must do so in spirit and truth.**

"God is a Spirit: and they that worship him must worship him in spirit and in truth" (John 4:24 KJV).

(A Psalm of David.) The LORD *is* my shepherd; I shall not want.

2 He maketh me to lie down in green pastures: he leadeth me beside the still waters.

3 He restoreth my soul: he leadeth me in the paths of righteousness for his name's sake.

4 Yea, though I walk through the valley of the shadow of death, I will fear no evil: for thou *art* with me; thy rod and thy staff they comfort me.

5 Thou preparest a table before me in the presence of mine enemies: thou anointest my head with oil; my cup runneth over.

6 Surely goodness and mercy shall follow me all the days of my life: and I will dwell in the house of the LORD for ever. (Psalms 23 KJV).

Now, let's go to Psalm 16:11 again.

"Thou wilt shew me the path of life: in thy presence *is* fulness of joy; at thy right hand *there are* pleasures for evermore" (Psalms 16:11 KJV).

So what we are going to talk about is being in the will of God. Jesus taught the disciples in Matthew 6:9-10 to pray in this manner.

"After this manner therefore pray ye: Our Father which art in heaven, Hallowed be thy name. Thy kingdom come. Thy will be done in earth, as *it is* in heaven" (Matthew 6:9-10 KJV).

Being in His presence is being in His Will. Because if you stay in His presence, He says I am going to show you the what? Paths of life. We want to comprehend these great scriptures because if we get it, we will have the God kind of life. He says out of all your getting, get understanding. "Wisdom *is* the principal thing; *therefore* get

wisdom: and with all thy getting get understanding"
(Proverbs 4:7 KJV).

If we get this in our spirit, we know that being in His
presence is life. And so, He said, at His right hand, thou
will show me the path of life. In Thy presence is fullness
of joy. He said at Thy right hand there are pleasures--with
an –s, for- evermore. So, it is not just short-term goodies,
but good things, holy things, right things--things that will
cause us to have the fullness of joy. We are in the world
but are not of it. So, things that bother the world ought
not to bother us: the people of God. We don't know that,
though, if we don't stay in His presence. So, we are going
to take it a step farther. And what I found of these
pleasures one of the pleasures at His right hand is <u>His will</u>.
The word "pleasure" "means a state of gratification; a
source of delight or joy" (Merriam Webster Online). "A

state of feeling of being pleased; enjoyment or satisfaction derived from what is to one's liking; delight; enjoyment; joy, refer to the feeling of being pleased and happy."

Pleasures, and He calls them good pleasures. Hallelujah. God is trying to get the church to be conformed to Him, to His Will. You know He doesn't want grudging givers. God wants cheerful givers.

Are you listening? ™

So, when it is time to enter into His presence, we need to decrease by entering into His Presence with praise, worship, and thanksgiving by praying in The Holy Spirit (some would say The Holy Ghost), which is your prayer language, which will take you to new levels of praise and worship. Hallelujah! Oh, Glory to God! Are you listening?

™   "Make a joyful noise unto the LORD, all ye lands" (Psalm 100:1 KJV). "Enter into his gates with

8

thanksgiving, and into his courts with praise: be thankful unto him, and bless his name" (Psalm 100:4 KJV).

I don't know if you really believe this or not, but when we enter into this place (the presence of God), through praise, worship, and thanksgiving, this is a place that God has ordained for us to be. So, therefore, it's something that we are to be excited about, because we're not only in His presence, but we are also in His Will. And His Will is one of those --Oh--pleasures that He has ordained. Now, we are going to talk about being in His Will. And we know that God has also given us a will.

Chapter 2: ILLUSTRATIONS OF BEING IN THE

WILL OF GOD

Let's talk about God's plan for mankind through Adam and Eve. Let's talk about the story of Adam and Eve in Genesis chapter 2 and chapter 3. In chapter 2, God said that it was not good for man to be alone. So, God completed Adam with his helpmate: his wife, Eve. We know through scripture that everything God made was good.

Genesis 2:16-25 KJV:

16 And the LORD God commanded the man, saying, Of every tree of the garden thou mayest freely eat:

17 But of the tree of the knowledge of good and evil, thou shalt not eat of it: for in the day that thou eatest thereof thou shalt surely die.

18 And the LORD God said, *It is* not good that the man

should be alone; I will make him an help meet for him.

19 And out of the ground the LORD God formed every beast of the field, and every fowl of the air; and brought *them* unto Adam to see what he would call them: and whatsoever Adam called every living creature, that *was* the name thereof.

20 And Adam gave names to all cattle, and to the fowl of the air, and to every beast of the field; but for Adam there was not found an help meet for him.

21 And the LORD God caused a deep sleep to fall upon Adam, and he slept: and he took one of his ribs, and closed up the flesh instead thereof;

22 And the rib, which the LORD God had taken from man, made he a woman, and brought her unto the man.

23 And Adam said, This *is* now bone of my bones, and flesh of my flesh: she shall be called Woman, because she was taken out of Man.

24 Therefore shall a man leave his father and his mother, and shall cleave unto his wife: and they shall be one flesh.

25 And they were both naked, the man and his wife, and were not ashamed.

So, here we see that when God made man, man was made in the presence of God. Man was made in the plan of God. And because God is all righteous, man was perfect. They could not see nakedness; they could not see ill will; they could not see sin because they were in the presence of God. And God is perfect, and they were covered in all areas by His presence. Because in God, there is no darkness—all light. And this is why we need to keep ourselves filled with the Word of God. Staying filled with the Word of God will keep you in the presence of God. Praying in the Holy Spirit, the language of the Holy Ghost, will keep you in the presence of God. Are you listening?™ I pray that you are being filled with these words for they are the Rhema Words of God. Let he that has ears to hear and eyes to see, hear what God is saying to the people of God.

In Christianity, *rhema* is used in Bible study to signify Jesus Christ's utterance. The Greek word *rhema* is useful to distinguish between two meanings of *word*. While both *rhema* and *logos* are translated into the English *word*, in the original Greek there was a substantial distinction ("Rhema" Wikipedia).

So, this is what He is talking about when we say—He wants us to say--Thy Will be done. We have a will; then, there is a will of the devil. Before all of that there is a will of God. And when we get to be *true* sons of the Father, we are going to want to surrender our will to Him, because surrendering your will to Him will cause Him to give it back to you. And you don't have peace like you have peace when you are walking in the will of God. You don't know what life is until the will of the Father has become your will. You will not even want a will of your own. You ought to want *Thy will be done* like Jesus said. Now, I am going to give you scriptures. When the will of the Father is in one's life, hey, there is nothing like it. I

mean, you are whole when in the will of the Father.

Luke 22:40-46 (KJV), with emphasis on verse 42

(...nevertheless not my will, but thine, be done):

40 And when he was at the place, he said unto them, Pray that ye enter not into temptation.

41 And he was withdrawn from them about a stone's cast, and kneeled down, and prayed,

42 Saying, Father, if thou be willing, remove this cup from me: nevertheless not my will, but thine, be done.

43 And there appeared an angel unto him from heaven, strengthening him.

44 And being in an agony he prayed more earnestly: and his sweat was as it were great drops of blood falling down to the ground.

45 And when he rose up from prayer, and was come to his disciples, he found them sleeping for sorrow,

46 And said unto them, Why sleep ye? rise and pray, lest ye enter into temptation.

"Saying, Father, if thou be willing, remove this cup from me: nevertheless not my will, but thine, be done" (Luke 22:42 KJV).

"Then answered Jesus and said unto them, Verily, verily, I say unto you, The Son can do nothing of himself, but what he seeth the Father do: for what things soever he doeth, these also doeth the Son likewise" (John 5:19 KJV).

"Then said Jesus unto them, When ye have lifted up the Son of man, then shall ye know that I am he, and that I do nothing of myself; but as my Father hath taught me, I speak these things" (John 8:28 KJV).

I am thinking about a few years ago when my daughter asked us if we wanted to go to Florida with her and her family. And she had asked me a couple of times already. And when she approached me the third time about this she asked, "Oh, you're not going?"

I said, "Yes, I am." And I said, "Yes, I am" before I had the opportunity to go to the Father." I don't want to go anywhere without being in the will of God. Because if I go with His will, in His will, I know it is going to be all good. So, having said that already, I had to go to the Father, and I had to ask for forgiveness.

Oh, Sister St. Clair, you are so silly, and some might even say helpless or needy. (Why do you always have to ask God everything?) If Jesus said He did nothing on His own, I want to be like Jesus. Why can't I ask? Getting back to the story of the trip to Florida with my daughter and her family, we were to leave that Friday going to Florida. We would always spend the night in Georgia somewhere around Marietta or Atlanta. On that Friday night, there was a horrible tornado and horrible weather. The tornado even hit the CNN station and tore up other

things in Atlanta. Some of you might even remember this.
If we had gone the way that we had originally planned,
which was that Friday, we more than likely would have
been in that tornadic weather, but because I prayed and
included God in my plans, He began to direct our path.
Therefore, we left on that Saturday and drove to Florida
in nice, bright sun-shinny weather.

"Trust in the LORD with all thine heart; and lean not
unto thine own understanding. In all thy ways
acknowledge him, and he shall direct thy paths. Be not
wise in thine own eyes..." (Proverbs 3:5-7 KJV).

You can call me what you want. But, I want to be in
the will of God. I don't want to travel all the way to
Florida—or any place else on these dangerous highways,
airways, railways in this dangerous, unsettled world--
without being in the will of God. Because if you are not
in His will, then you are in some other kind of will. And

anything can happen. But, if you are in His will, He knows

how to move everything else out of the way.

Isaiah 55:8-11 KJV

8 For my thoughts *are* not your thoughts, neither *are* your ways my ways, saith the LORD.

9 For *as* the heavens are higher than the earth, so are my ways higher than your ways, and my thoughts than your thoughts.

10 For as the rain cometh down, and the snow from heaven, and returneth not thither, but watereth the earth, and maketh it bring forth and bud, that it may give seed to the sower, and bread to the eater:

11 So shall my word be that goeth forth out of my mouth: it shall not return unto me void, but it shall accomplish that which I please, and it shall prosper *in the thing* whereto I sent it.

The old folks say, God knows how to remove all

obstacles out of our way before we get there. I'm so glad I

prayed that prayer. As we were going to be leaving on that

Friday, I felt lead in my spirit to keep watching the

weather. And you know? The weather was just acting up, and it had been acting up. The weather has been unusual ever since then. But, let me tell you what happens when you invite God into your travel and you pray, LORD, not my will, but Your will be done. God knows how to create a path for you. Are you listening? See, this may not be important to you, but it is important to me. I once had a lady who is now a big-time preacher ask me: You pray about everything, don't you? About every place you go?

And I said, "Yes, I try to." When I find myself not doing that, then I know that I am not tight with God like I ought to be. See, I mean she wasn't condemning me or anything. She said, You know, I've never done that.

But, I hope that gave her food for thought. Because you can't be no preacher, and especially a pastor, if you don't pray the will of God in your life. Because if you are a pastor, then you are not walking in His will--not necessary walking in His will, not necessarily walking in His plans, which is one of the pleasures in His right hand. So, there is a possibility you're leading a whole bunch of people down the *wrong* road. I once had a lady say to me (she's gone on to be with Jesus now) and she was very anointed. She would just hop from church to church.

And one night we were talking on the phone; first, she asked me to pray and ask God what church she was supposed to be in. That is what we were talking about at that time. She requested of me, "Will you pray and ask God Where am I supposed to be?" And I acted like I did not hear her because we had just started the church. So, before the conversation was over, she asked again: Did you hear what I said? I asked if you would pray and ask God where I am supposed to be. She said you know I have gone to many churches, but I'm not sure that I have ever been in the right one because I've never prayed and asked God.

And you know I'm not condemning her because a lot of us are like that. Even though we pretty much know when we are home, but some people are home and get up and leave home. Because they don't know the will of God. And if you are in the will of God, if you want to be in that church or not, you will hang tight because that is the Will of God. That is one of His pleasures. I mean that is a good pleasure to be where God wants you to be.

I was reading in The Bible where Jesus had to pray three times. I will take you to the scriptures. But every time He entered into prayer, He said not my will but Your Will be done.

Notes:

_____

_____

_____

_____

_____

_____

_____

Chapter 3: THIS IS WHAT HAPPENS WHEN YOU PRAY

Matthew 26:39-44 KJV

39 And he went a little further, and fell on his face, and prayed, saying, O my Father, if it be possible, let this cup pass from me: nevertheless not as I will, but as thou *wilt*.

40 And he cometh unto the disciples, and findeth them asleep, and saith unto Peter, What, could ye not watch with me one hour?

41 Watch and pray, that ye enter not into temptation: the spirit indeed *is* willing, but the flesh *is* weak. (The natural man versus the Spirit of God.)

42 He went away again the second time, and prayed, saying, O my Father, if this cup may not pass away from

23

me, except I drink it, thy will be done.

43 And he came and found them asleep again: for their eyes were heavy.

44 And he left them, and went away again, and prayed the third time, saying the same words.

So, I prayed, and remember, she asked me to pray. I prayed right in her ears, so she could agree with me. The next day or so, she had given me some money to go buy some carpet for our first church for the platform. I was out getting that carpet, and when I got home, before I could unlock the door, I could hear the phone ringing. And it was her. While I was getting the carpet, God spoke to me to tell her something. I tried to ignore it.

God said, "Tell her to come and help you and Robert build." I wanted to ignore that because I could have easily thought that myself. We just started a church, and *she* did not know where she belonged; even though, she was in a church. So, you know how sometimes God just bugs you to do something? He kept bugging me. I kept trying to ignore Him. I didn't want to hear that. Because I had already figured out she is going to think it's me. He kept on bugging me. So, I said well, if you want me to tell her, you have her to call me. I guess He said, If that is the way you want it, you go home because before you open the door the phone is going to be ringing. It is going to be her. I could hear the phone ringing on the outside of the door. I went in racing and picked up the phone. It *was* her. So quite natural after we got through our hellos, I told her what God said. And before then, we were friends, and it was "Yes, girl…" to me.

Right after I gave her that message it was "Yes, ma'am," from that day on until she went home to be with

Jesus. "Yes, ma'am," (it had a little edge on it—a little chill on it). Yes, ma'am, she would say, hostile--upset with me. You asked me; I told her. You said you had never asked God where you belonged. See, my husband and I had left a church at the leading of God and started our own ministry. And we left the church in good standing with our Pastor. (We could always go back to that church with our heads up and not down because we left the right way.) We had been praying for years: should we go? at least once a year.

As the song goes, should we stay, or should we go? At least we didn't just jump up and walk out. And every year, He'd bring us the same answer: Stand still-- meaning don't go nowhere. And I am glad we did not just jump up and move. Because that is where our ministry was in a sense founded and grounded. Are you listening? ™ So, we stayed. If we had just jumped up and did it, we would have messed up what God is doing with us right now. We would have missed God. Are you listening? ™

So, what my friend that asked me to pray about which church she should be going to did: got an attitude with me. She got into the flesh. I mean, she never said, "Yes, girl" anymore after that. She's gone home to be with Jesus now. Before she went to be with Jesus, one day she worked up the nerve to ask me: "Why did God tell you and didn't tell me?" I said because you asked me to pray. But what she didn't know--He told me when He was calling me into ministry: there will be many prayers of others He wouldn't answer. But when you ask Me, I'll answer. Don't ask me why? Ask Him. God told me that, and I've watched it over the years. He does just that.

She said, "Well, I just don't understand why He did not tell me." I said, you asked me to pray. Now, she would not have been that hostile toward me if He had told her to go to some big, fabulous church. She would have been hugging me, probably would have given me another offering. But, excuse me. God is telling me to come help you?

"Therefore said he unto them, The harvest truly is great, but the labourers are few: pray ye therefore the Lord of the harvest, that he would send forth labourers into his harvest" (Luke 10:2 KJV).

Well, look. God needs you to be positioned where you can help. There is no reason to go to another church that is already overflowing with help and doesn't have room in their bank accounts because they have all the money they need. You want to go somewhere and take credit for

something you didn't do. Hey! I'm going to size this up

with scriptures. He was telling her: Come help them build.

"Whatsoever thy hand findeth to do, do it with thy

might; for there is no work, nor device, nor knowledge,

nor wisdom, in the grave, whither thou

goest"(Ecclesiastes 9:10 KJV).

"I must work the works of him that sent me, while it is

day: the night cometh, when no man can work"(John

9:4 KJV).

Notes:

_____

_____

_____

_____

Chapter 4: IT TAKES TOOLS TO BUILD AND GOD WANTS CHEERFUL GIVERS

How many of you know if you are helping someone to build, you are going to have a hammer in your hand, and nails, and an axe, and other tools? In other words, when you are helping someone to build, you have work to do. And I say, God wants a cheerful giver. God doesn't want us dragging our feet.

Oh well, church starts at eleven. Umm, I'll get there by eleven-thirty. What are you trying to miss? What you *are* missing is something that is going to get you into the presence of God like praise and worship. Uh. If you are supposed to be at church at a certain time, you should get there at least thirty to fifteen minutes before that time, so you can be positioned so that God can speak to you. Dragging, coming when you want to--you're not being a cheerful giver. You are not missing a slice of the pie; you are missing the whole pie.

Well, you don't have to believe me because if I have time, I am going to bring it through the Word. If God sees fit for me to say it, I am still going to *Blow the Trumpet and Sound the Alarm.*™ (Go to stclamin.org and click on www.faithtalkstl.com).

Are you listening? ™

We want to do fabulous things and just want to do it our way. We don't want to be in the will of God. We would be surprised when God calls for those who thought they were in His will. We would be surprised who are going to be left behind. Oh, Jesus! And believe it or not, a lot of those who are going to be left behind are sitting in the pews every Sunday. They'd tell you if the Word is not going the way they want it to go, if things are not going the way they want them to go, they would just jump up and do something different and be out of the will of God. And they would be one of those that He was speaking of when He said depart from Me you workers of iniquity. I know you not.

"But he shall say, I tell you, I know you not whence ye are; depart from me, all ye workers of iniquity" (Luke 13:27).

But, God, I sang songs in the church. I gave all of my money because You was always asking for it. But, He's looking for people; He's looking for sons; He's looking for servants that will be disciplined to His will.

See, when you are slothful (lazy, idle, inactive like a sloth), and as the old folk would call it, when you are slow footing, when you are dragging your feet, and when you are doing

things the way you want to do it, that is not

showing God love. That's being rebellious. "For

rebellion is as the sin of witchcraft, and

stubbornness is as iniquity and idolatry. Because

thou has rejected the word of the LORD, he

hath also rejected thee from being king." (I

Samuel 15:23 KJV). That's just like if you would

tell your child to do something, and your child

does it when he or she wants to do it. You tell

them, come on get over here, and they take their

time, and you mean business if it is no more

than pulling their ear or just snatching them.

Nobody ever did that but me. Ha Ha. You

know, you did something to let them know,

when I say something, you respect what I say,

and you do it. I don't care if you are not ready to do what I say. I'm ready for you to do it. That's enough. Hello? Not, Oh baby, you are dragging your feet because you are not ready to do it. Oh, bless you. Go back and sit down.

That's the way Daphine does my husband. Daphine is our little girl (our little Shih Tzu). When it is time to take her out to wee wee, now, she's the one that's got to wee wee, he says, "Come on, Daphine." He's got a certain time that he takes her out. And you know, she loves for him to beg her like she's his wife, like he's her husband. You know how some of you wives get: you don't do it my way; you have to beg me. He said, "Come on, Daphine." Now, she knows when he says, "Come on, Daphine" and heads for the washroom she is supposed to be right behind him, so she can get on her leash. So, she can go out. But what she'll do, she'll come out far enough for him to see her. She'll drag, and then she'll sit. And he'll have to walk from the washroom to where she is. Unless he says, "Come on, Daphine, Come on!" He changes the tone of his voice, and then she just takes her time. Ha Ha. She got that little woman spirit in her—that little wife spirit. I say, Hey! That is my husband, Daphine! I mean, she knows what he is saying because she sticks her head out like this—her neck. Hook me up, but you're going to have to walk to me to hook me up. Take me out to *pee*. Ha Ha. Are you listening? ™

Well, see, that is the way we do God. HE said come and get under the <u>wings of My Will</u>. And you are d-r-a-g-g-i-n-g your feet. I'll get there about 11:30. You want me, God? You need me over there?

If you think HE needs you so bad, you mess around and die. And see how quickly your position gets filled. I mean--I don't` know if you all noticed this or not--but people don't cry over you too long once you are dead. I don't care how much they love you, there is something about having your funeral and putting you in the ground gives one strength to get to the next day. And there's nothing wrong with that healing process because we can always keep them in our memories. But, it just kinda shows you, we do need God. Amen? We need to be disciplined to the will of God. You know, it is a beautiful day out there today. Beautiful! Like David said: "This [is] the day [which] the LORD hath made; we will rejoice and be glad in it" (Psalms 118:24 KJV).

You would think it is raining and snowing with the

people of God every worship day because they take

that day to do whatever they want to do with it. God,

would it be ok if I go to my scriptures? Paul says, "Not

forsaking the assembling of yourselves together, as the

manner of some is; but exhorting one another: and so

much the more, as ye see the day approaching"

(Hebrews 10:25 KJV). Are you listening? ™

> Teaching was needed in Paul's day to help the
> members of the church realize that they must
> not neglect their worship to the Lord.
> Apparently there were some who were
> rebellious, and others who were careless and
> indifferent, just as there are today. We can profit
> from Paul's teaching, if we will listen to him.
> (Excerpted from "Forsaking the Assembling"
> by Paul O. Nichols in The Christian Informer,
> September, 1997).

Let us stop and think for a moment and ask ourselves

this question: Am I in the will of God? Are you

listening?^{TM} Oh, Sisters and Brothers, That's ok. Let's

not fight about it. I was just trying to give you word for

thought--something to think about.

See, lots of times when a question like this comes,

you almost feel like pastor is putting a heavy on you.

But, this is not supposed to weight you down. This is

supposed to free you up to know when you are in the

will of God you are in good hands. Are you listening?

^{TM} Not only are you in good hands, but it is like being

locked up in a place that you love to be. You know, a

person that eats a lot, I don't think they mind being

locked up in a grocery store or an all-you-can-eat soul

food buffet.

A person that loves to steal, you have people that

would steal the color off of red. You have some people that l- o- v- e to steal, and I guarantee a thief that steals will go into a store weighing 120 pounds comes out weighing 220 pounds. I don't think they would mind being locked up in a clothing store because that is going to give them an opportunity to really steal.

Now, to be in the will of God is being 1. where we should desire to be, 2. where He wants us to be, 3. where we need to be. And the reason that you don't want to be in His will is because you think it is a horrible place to be.

The Word of God teaches us in St. John 3:16-21 that God so loved us that He gave His Son (Jesus) for us not to condemn us or to make us feel bad, but when we reject His Word for us, the Word of God comes to us twice through Jesus who is the Word and through the written word. And when we reject what the written Word says (The Holy Bible) because what the person of the Word (Jesus) did, when we reject that, then we are rejecting the Will of God. Please read this with an open heart:

16 For God so loved the world, that he gave his only begotten Son, that whosoever believeth in him should not perish, but have everlasting life.

17 For God sent not his Son into the world to condemn the world; but that the world through him might be saved.

18 He that believeth on him is not condemned: but he that believeth not is condemned already, because he hath not believed in the name of the only begotten Son

of God.

19 And this is the condemnation, that light is come into the world, and men loved darkness rather than light, because their deeds were evil.

20 For every one that doeth evil hateth the light, neither cometh to the light, lest his deeds should be reproved.

21 But he that doeth truth cometh to the light, that his deeds may be made manifest, that they are wrought in God. (John 3:16-21 KJV).

But there are some things, if you really get to know what they are, you will love them. Because it is going to give you the opportunity to be everything 1. you ought to be, 2. you should be, 3. when you need to be.

Are you listening? ™

Chapter 5: NOT MY WILL BUT THY WILL BE DONE

Thy will be done, not mine but Thine will be done. Go to Matthew chapter 6. Hallelujah. The disciples asked Jesus, how do we pray? What must we say when we pray? And then, praying is just not words. We must have faith in what we are praying. Praying is not just saying but having faith in what you are saying. Hallelujah! He went on to tell them:

6 But thou, when thou prayest, enter into thy closet, and when thou hast shut thy door, pray to thy Father which is in secret; and thy Father which seeth in secret shall reward thee openly.

7 But when ye pray, use not vain repetitions, as the heathen do: for they think that they shall be heard for their much speaking.

8 Be not ye therefore like unto them: for your Father knoweth what things ye have need of, before ye ask him.

9 After this manner therefore pray ye: Our Father which art in heaven, Hallowed be thy name.

10 Thy kingdom come. Thy will be done in earth, as it is in heaven.

11 Give us this day our daily bread.

12 And forgive us our debts, as we forgive our debtors.

13 And lead us not into temptation, but deliver us from evil: For thine is the kingdom, and the power, and the glory, for ever. Amen.

Verse 10 is our key verse:

"Thy kingdom come. Thy will be done in earth, as *it is* in heaven" (Matthew 6:10 KJV). Jesus says in earth, in Me, because we are not in the earth; we are on the earth. We are earthen vessels. Oh, Jesus. We are earthen vessels. Thy will be done in me--as it is in Heaven.

So, Jesus said to the disciples this is how you pray. You ask God. God, let Your Will be done in me even as it is in Heaven--even as it is with You. I dare you to pray that prayer and *mean* that prayer. See, God knows when you ask stuff and you mean it. But, ask that of God and *mean* it. And allow Him to work His will in you. You will become one of the most peaceful, happiest persons you have ever known. That doesn't mean that you are not going to be tempted to want to do it your way. But because you have asked God, you will also be strengthened, and God will give you the understanding to know, well, you know: God, it is not all about me. It is about You. So, I mean it's nothing wrong with asking that just simply because God is bringing this to us today. If we are doing things on our own, we should start asking God: Let Your will be done in me even as it is in Heaven.

Hallelujah! The Bible says we have to work out our own salvation. He said *soul s*alvation with fear and trembling. You don't know how it is going to turn out. But, you know what? Do it anyway. My Mama used to say: Hey, baby, you don't want to get too close to God. If you get too close to God, you'll die. So what if I die. I'm close to God. It has got to be better in Heaven than it is down here. It has got to be all good. Are you listening? ™

Somebody said, Oh, Sister St. Clair, I don't want you to die. What I am saying is somebody has given her the wrong info because God says in His Word: Draw nigh to Me, and I will draw night to you. (See James 4:7 KJV.) God said, if you want to get closer to Me, I'll get closer to you. Glory! That's what He said.

I mean--you know what the LORD revealed to me? HE said the reason that the church is in such turmoil--the reason that we are in such trouble--I mean actually experiencing it is because HE tells us in John chapter 16:33. In this world, we are going to have trails and tribulation. HE said be of good cheer: I have already overcome the world. "These things I have spoken unto you, that in me ye might have peace. In the world ye shall have tribulation: but be of good cheer; I have overcome the world" (John 16:33 KJV).

What HE is saying is don't be afraid.

"Yea, though I walk through the valley of the shadow of death, I will fear no evil: for thou art with me; thy rod and thy staff they comfort me" (Psalm 23:4 KJV).

Why? Because you are with me, God. Hallelujah. And all that I can't handle, You will handle it. And You keep me in perfect peace because I am in Your presence. Glory!

CHAPTER 6: PUT ON THE GARMENT OF PRAISE FOR THE SPIRIT OF HEAVINESS

To appoint unto them that mourn in Zion, to give unto them beauty for ashes, the oil of joy for mourning, the garment of praise for the spirit of heaviness; that they might be called trees of righteousness, the planting of the LORD, that he might be glorified. (Isaiah 61:3 KJV).

Yes, it's good. It is better than what you are having for dinner tonight. This is your chicken and dressing right here. Glory! I am trying to stop hollering, but there's a praise on the inside that I can't keep to myself…See, that's what I am talking about right there! Yeah! I am trying to be nice. Hey! But there is just something about being in

His Presence. There is just something about being in His Will. Yes! Every now and again, honey, you get the hook up! You can't do *nothing* but praise Him! Yes! Yes! *All of the Glory goes to God!*

And I bet some of you didn't even think you felt good until you got into His presence and all of a sudden that thing had to *bow* to the *Presence* of God. That situation had to *bow* to His presence. Yes! Glory! That's what the man is saying; a holler coming up that I can't keep to myself! Glory! There's something about being in *His Presence,* something about being in His will! Yes! Let's try to get on with this.

So, Jesus said, Thy Kingdom come. This is how you are supposed to pray: Thy will be done in me even as it is in heaven. I dare you to give that a try. Stop trying to help God out. What I was going to say: God said the reason we have so much trouble--the reason there is so much division in the homes, the reason there are so many problems in the churches' finances and in your personal finances is because you won't let the will of God be done. See, we want to have 100-fold peace. Let's say, 100-fold perfectness. One hundred-fold maturity in the things of God, but we won't give Him our will. And so, if we keep our will from out of *His* will, we are going to have trouble just like the world. We are going to experience the same kind of problems; we are going to be defeated because He said we are in the world but not of it. And what that means is you are in every kind of trouble there is in the world. But, this the key, because you are not of it. HE said, only with your eyes will you behold it.

That is what He tells us in Psalm 91.

5 Thou shalt not be afraid for the terror by night;

nor for the arrow *that* flieth by day;

6 *Nor* for the pestilence *that* walketh in darkness; *nor* for the destruction *that* wasteth at noonday.

7 A thousand shall fall at thy side, and ten thousand at thy right hand; *but* it shall not come nigh thee.

8 Only with thine eyes shalt thou behold and see the reward of the wicked.

9 Because thou hast made the LORD, *which is* my refuge, *even* the most High, thy habitation;

10 There shall no evil befall thee, neither shall any plague come nigh thy dwelling. (Psalms 91: 5-10 KJV).

But, you know when you are not in the will of God,

you are going to behold more than with the eyes. You are
going to be defeated in areas of your life just like the
world (unbelievers). You might lose your house like they
lose their houses in the world. You might lose your car
like they lose their cars in the world. You might become
sick and die of certain things like they do in the world.
Why? Because you are not allowing that good pleasure:
The will of God. You are not partaking of it. I am not
saying that these things are going to happen to you, I am
just saying it is better to be under the covering of His will
than out of His will. This is not to put fear in you, I am
just Blowing the Trumpet and Sounding the Alarm. I hope
that you hear what my heart is saying as a preacher woman
of God. In The Lord's Prayer, Jesus taught His disciples
to pray Thy Will be done in me as it is in Heaven. The
Bible tells us that it rains on the just as well as the unjust.

But it is better to be in His will even if it rains on us the just.

Many of our young adults are looking for husbands and wives and have asked God for them, but they jump ahead of God, um, jumping ahead of God, doing it their way and want God to smile on it. God *does not* bless mess. But if you *wait* on God!--I will never forget the testimony of a well-known Christian artist. She had become a woman of a very mature age by then. Um. I know she's older than me. And I was with her one night in her dressing room. She was here in St. Louis, and I was one of the singers that was on her ticket that night. They put me on her program, and I sung one of my songs. And after the concert, I went into her dressing room with her. She had asked me back there because I wanted to speak with her. She said come in. Just come on back to my dressing room. I went into her dressing room where she was. And I am telling you this one thing: she got on the phone with her husband. I don't know who called who, either her husband called her, or she called her husband. And you would have thought they were teenagers. She did not get married until she was a very mature woman of age, but she waited on God! I could not hear what her husband was saying, but I heard what she was saying. I heard her speaking all that sweet lovey dovey stuff.

See, if you're going to be in the will of God, if you are going to ask God for something, then you are going to have to wait on Him. Look, He is not trying to work the kinks out of your mate, He is trying to work the kinks out of you. But if you try to help Him, you are messing up the whole thing. I heard on the TV yesterday, a well-known singer got married and had this big, fabulous wedding, and they have been living together since 2002.

But the church does the same thing. They are living together unmarried, they are in the church, they are singing in the choir, and some of them are even preaching. They are working on the usher board, and then all of a sudden, they want to throw a big wedding. They are living together and want to wear white. They should not have anything like white on but black, dark gray, deepest purple anything but white. (Smile.)

Because white represents purity, and that is not purity because you went ahead of God. I am talking to saved folks. The world is supposed to do stuff like that because they don't know any better.

The Bible says, we are to bring our flesh under subjection.

But I keep under my body, and bring *it* into subjection:

lest that by any means, when I have preached to others, I myself should be a castaway. (1 Corinthians 9:27 KJV.)

But I discipline my body and keep it under control, lest after preaching to others I myself should be disqualified. (1 Corinthians 9:27 ESV.)

Instead, I discipline my body and bring it under strict control, so that after preaching to others, I myself will not be disqualified.

(1 Corinthians 9:27 CSB.)

And what is that? Under control, but since it seems you don't have any control, which means self-discipline (which we do through the power of the Holy Spirit) then you should put it under the blood of Jesus Christ. You cast down those imaginations. You tell that body: I can wait. I will be disciplined. I'm not just waiting on a man. I'm not just waiting on a woman. I'm waiting on my man (if you are a woman). I'm waiting on my woman (if you are a man). Yes. You will be surprised who is sleeping with who. Let's get to the scriptures.

2 Corinthians 10:3-6 KJV:

3 For though we walk in the flesh, we do not war after the flesh:

4 (For the weapons of our warfare *are* not carnal, but mighty through God to the pulling down of strong holds;)

5 Casting down imaginations, and every high thing that exalteth itself against the knowledge of God, and bringing into captivity every thought to the obedience of Christ;

6 And having in a readiness to revenge all disobedience, when your obedience is fulfilled.

Ok, watch out now, Brother. How long have you been married? Umm. Let's not get any *d -e -e -p -e -r* (sung in musical tone ♫).

When you are feeling like you can't do it, you're not going to make it, you're restless, burdened down with the cares of life, lift up your head and your hands and begin to tell GOD how good HE is, how Almighty HE is, how much you love HIM, how much you need HIM, open your mouth and begin to sing and say praises unto our GOD. This is what you call putting on the garment of praise for the spirit of heaviness. Hallelujah! Glory to God. Thank you, Jesus.

That heaviness that you are carrying have got to leave. Amen.

Chapter 7: GOD HAS NOT GIVEN US A SPIRIT OF FEAR BUT POWER, LOVE, AND A SOUND MIND

HE said: Thy will be done in me as it is in Heaven. Go with me to Matthew chapter 26 verse 36. Jesus prayed three times because the spirit of fear--the weight of the world had begun to descend upon Jesus. It was fear. He did not want to experience that type of pain: all of *our* sins.

Then cometh Jesus with them unto a place called Gethsemane, and saith unto the disciples, Sit ye here, while I go and pray yonder. And he took with him Peter and the two sons of Zebedee, and began to be sorrowful and very heavy. Then saith he unto them, My soul is exceeding sorrowful, even unto death: tarry ye here, and watch with me. And he went a little farther, and fell on his face, and prayed, saying, O my Father, if it be possible, let this cup pass from me: nevertheless not as I will, but as thou wilt.

(Matthew 26:36-39 KJV)

Jesus *is* such a loving Savior. And what He wants us to know there is no temptation that is tempting you in any area that He has not already given you a way out of. Jesus is saying He has been there. He did not become Almighty until He had defeated death. So, everything that He had experienced at the point of His death and resurrection, He was experiencing it as we now experience it. But guess what? He was experiencing it in the will of God, which gave Him the ability to go through with it. He gave up His life--by the way--they *did not* take His life.

"There hath no temptation taken you but such as is

common to man: but God is faithful, who will not

suffer you to be tempted above that ye are able; but

will with the temptation also make a way to escape,

that ye may be able to bear it"

(1 Corinthians 10:13 KJV).

That is why He says in Matthew 26 verse 39: Oh, my

Father, it if be possible, let this cup pass from me.

Nevertheless, not as I want it to be, but as You want it to

be. Not my will, but Yours.

40: And he cometh unto the disciples, and findeth them

asleep, and saith unto Peter, What, could ye not watch

with me one hour?" (Matthew 26:40 KJV).

In other words, you know how you have certain

people that you depend on to help you to pray through?

(They were praying through all right.) (LOL). *Their will was*

definitely at work; they went to sleep. What God is trying to show us is we are empowered by God to work His will. And if you do not ever spend time with God, if you don't come before Him as one of his children, you are not going to be empowered. If you are always missing church, never hearing the Word preached, I want you to know preaching will keep you alive, not just reading The Bible. If you are unable to attend a church, you can always listen to right preaching through radio, tv, and the internet: YouTube and Facebook. There are so many ways you can find a good, right, saved, Holy Ghost filled Bible-teaching preacher. This is what HE is saying when the Bible says: How then shall they call on him in whom they have not believed? and how shall they believe in him of whom they have not heard? and how shall they hear without a preacher? And how shall they preach, except they be sent? as it is written, How beautiful are the feet of them that preach the gospel of peace, and bring glad tidings of good things! (Romans 10:14-15 KJV) How can they hear except there be a preacher and how can he preach except he be sent? Are you listening? ™

If you are always staying out of His presence, there is no way that you can be in His Will. So, they were asleep because that is what flesh does. The flesh sleeps. The flesh is a dead work, by the way. See, Jesus did not come to save our flesh; He has come to save our spirits. Glory! GOD is the Father of spirits.

"Furthermore, we have had fathers of our flesh which corrected us, and we gave them reverence: shall we not much rather be in subjection unto the Father of spirits, and live?" (Hebrews 12:9 KJV).

Also "God is a Spirit: and they that worship him must worship him in spirit and in truth" (John 4:24 KJV).

According to John 17:17 KJV: "Sanctify them through thy truth: thy word is truth."

Jesus has come to save our spirits not our flesh. Our flesh is going back to the dust from which it came. So, flesh was sleeping; it had never been born again--let alone being filled with the Spirit.

"Watch and pray, that ye enter not into temptation: the spirit indeed is willing, but the flesh is weak" (Matthew 26:41 KJV).

He is saying be attentive. There is always something out there to minister to your spirit telling you why you can do it yourself (without God). Remember when you were a little child, or you had a little child who walked around with his or her shoes on the wrong feet and wearing their coat upside down, when someone would try to help the child get it right, the child throws a tantrum. Come here; let me help you. The child screams and does not want help. I was working at our computer at home, and my husband came into the room, and he had on one of his house shoes and one of mine, and I was cracking up laughing, and all he would do was smile. But then I looked down and realized I had one of mine on one foot and one of his on the other. I tell you: I was so tickled; they were very comfortable. And on top of that, I had them on the wrong feet! My feet were so covered up. (Ha ha ha ha ha) See, my husband already knew I had on one of his shoes, and that's why he kept on parading around in front of me. He knew that I was going to be the one to open my mouth and tell him that he had done something wrong. All he said when I opened my mouth to say something was "look down." I could say nothing else just laugh, and so we exchanged shoes and went about our day. Getting back to the scripture: verse 41.

"Watch and pray, that ye enter not into temptation: the spirit indeed is willing, but the flesh is weak" (Matthew 26:41 KJV).

How many of you want to do it God's way? You have a desire. I know; me, too. You have a desire to do it God's way. You know it is not like it is in your heart to do wrong or not to obey God. It is just that any time you come out of the presence of God your flesh becomes weak. That is why we have to stay full of His Spirit. We have to understand and know that we are His. We belong to Him. We are not of this world. We are in the world but not of it. "If ye were of the world, the world would love his own: but because ye are not of the world, but I have chosen you out of the world, therefore the world hateth you" (John 15:19 KJV).

And the Holy Spirit on the inside of us will lead and guide us in the way that we should go.

The flesh is weak. This is why Jesus keeps praying. Verse 42 He went away again the second time. This means He did not throw up His hands and say forget about it. So that means, if we need to go back again, we go back again and get some help. If we need to hear this message again, we open up our hearts to hear it and gain strength from the Word of God.

"He went away again the second time, and prayed, saying, O my Father, if this cup may not pass away from me, except I drink it, thy will be done" (Matthew 26:42 KJV).

God, regardless to what I am feeling right now, *greater*

is He that is in me than he that is in the world. I don't care what kind of temptation comes your way to get you out of the will of God, we must realize, God's will for our lives is much better than our will that we personally want to walk in (doing it our own way). The Bible says, according to Jeremiah 29:11NIV: "For I know the plans I have for you, declares the LORD, plans to prosper you and not to harm you, plans to give you hope and a future."

CHAPTER 8: THE NATURAL MAN WARS AGAINST THE SPIRIT OF GOD

Hallelujah. You know, God has a will and a plan for where we live in the earth right now. Sometimes, oh, it is a fact, the flesh always wants something that it should not have or *cannot* handle later. Because the flesh wanna feel good.

"For the flesh lusteth against the Spirit, and the Spirit against the flesh: and these are contrary the one to the other: so that ye cannot do the things that ye would" (Galatians 5:17 KJV).

I don't know why we are under the mentality that feeling good is the right thing or the right way. Feeling good is not always the right path to travel. As a matter of fact, you had better watch it when you start feeling too good. Because something might be waiting on you around the corner. Let this mind that be in God be also in you. So, the scripture says:

"Let this mind be in you, which was also in Christ Jesus" (Philippians 2:5 KJV).

"And be renewed in the spirit of your mind;" (Ephesians 4:23 KJV).

"Because the carnal mind is enmity against God: for it is not subject to the law of God, neither indeed can be" (Romans 8:7 KJV).

"He went away again the second time, and prayed, saying, O my Father, if this cup may not pass away from me, except I drink it, thy will be done" (Matthew 26:42 KJV).

Verse 43

"And he came and found them asleep again: for their eyes

were heavy" (Matthew 26:43 KJV).

Because they were in the flesh. You cannot pay attention to what God is doing when you are in the *flesh*. And when you are in your will, *you are in the flesh!!* I am not talking to people that are in the world, I am talking about church people. I am talking about people that are called by His name. They were asleep again because their eyes were heavy. Oops, you did it again. Remember that song? (*Oops, I Did It Again*). You didn't intend to do that again. Well, I am just going to go ahead and be the person that I am. You didn't intend to commit fornication again. But you were at the wrong place, at the wrong time, with the right person. You must never be alone with a person that arouses your flesh; you should at least be with a chaperon. This will keep you from compromising your life of sanctification through sexual sin.

The Bible says:

15 Love not the world, neither the things that are in the world. If any man love the world, the love of the Father is not in him.

16 For all that is in the world, the lust of the flesh, and the lust of the eyes, and the pride of life, is not of the Father, but is of the world.

17 And the world passeth away, and the lust thereof: but he that doeth the will of God abideth for ever. (I John 2:15-17 KJV)

The Bible says all have sinned and have fallen short of the Glory of God.

20 Therefore by the deeds of the law there shall no flesh be justified in his sight: for by the law *is* the knowledge of sin. 21 But now the righteousness of God without the law is manifested, being witnessed by the law and the

prophets; <u>22</u> Even the righteousness of God *which is* by faith of Jesus Christ unto all and upon all them that believe: for there is no difference: <u>23</u> **For all have sinned, and come short of the glory of God;** <u>24</u> Being justified freely by his grace through the redemption that is in Christ Jesus: <u>25</u> Whom God hath set forth *to be* a propitiation through faith in his blood, to declare his righteousness for the remission of sins that are past, through the forbearance of God; <u>26</u> To declare, *I say*, at this time his righteousness: that he might be just, and the justifier of him which believeth in Jesus. (Romans 3:20-26 KJV).

Also, the scripture tells us that there is no temptation that has taken us but that such is common to man, but God has given us a way of escape.

"There hath no temptation taken you but such as is common to man: but God *is* faithful, who will not suffer you to be tempted above that ye are able; but will with the temptation also make a way to escape, that ye may be able to bear *it*"

(I Corinthians 10:13 KJV).

But let's say you are planning on getting married. If you are a man and are planning to marry a woman or you are a woman who is planning on marrying a man, then save yourself for each other and escape the sin of fornication. Stay away from stuff—whatever it may be that will cause you to compromise your relationship with God. Don't compromise your life of sanctification through Christ for a few minutes of pleasure, especially if it goes against the Word of God, the Will of God for our lives.

Because how many know flesh will make you try to do things that are wrong in front of people? And you are thinking they don't see, and you are the one that is asleep. I hope I am preaching. You are the one that is sleeping, not them. That is just like people getting drunk, drinking a lot of alcohol, and they don't smell like it when they get around others. But, you can look at a person's lips, look at the eyes, look at the skin and can tell when a person has a problem with alcohol. I'm not going to condemn you because that is between you and God if you want to continue getting drunk having no control over your consumption 😉.

I don't mean to judge, but you are probably addicted and feel that there is no way out. I can tell you this: God can and will deliver you from alcohol and from any addiction or stronghold if you want to be delivered.

According to Ephesians 6:12 KJV, the Word of God says this: "For we wrestle not against flesh and blood, but against principalities, against powers, against the rulers of the darkness of this world, against spiritual wickedness in high *places*."

Are you listening?™

And that's just like a person that smokes and wants to quit smoking. Lord, I don't want to continue smoking. Lord, please help me to quit smoking in Jesus' name. You don't have to ask Him please help just ask Him to help you to quit smoking in Jesus' name. And God will do it. Paul tells us in Philippians 4:6-7 be careful for nothing but in everything through prayer and supplication with thanksgiving we should let our requests be made known unto God, and the peace of God which surpasses all understanding will keep our hearts and minds through Christ Jesus. According to Philippians 4:6-9 KJV:

6 Be careful for nothing; but in every thing by prayer and supplication with thanksgiving let your requests be made known unto God.

7 And the peace of God, which passeth all understanding, shall keep your hearts and minds through Christ Jesus.

8 Finally, brethren, whatsoever things are true, whatsoever things *are* honest, whatsoever things *are* just, whatsoever things *are* pure, whatsoever things *are* lovely, whatsoever things *are* of good report; if *there be* any virtue, and if *there be* any praise, think on these things.

9 Those things, which ye have both learned, and received, and heard, and seen in me, do: and the God of peace shall be with you.

God will help you if you get rid of the cigarettes and don't go buy more. But there is no need of putting them in the church trash barrel and then going around the corner, paying five dollars for a pack. And you know you don't want to throw away the five dollars. Well, I'm just getting off of track here. But you are going to hang around stuff and things that you don't want to get rid of.

Oh, Lord, help me. Catch me, Holy Ghost, catch me. You stay in the will of God. The Bible says, shun even the appearance of evil.

"Abstain from all appearance of evil" (I Thessalonians 5:22 KJV).

So what did Jesus say? Oh, God, here they are asleep again. Here I am--don't want to die, don't want to go through all of this because of flesh. But, then you know what? There was more of God in Him than flesh. That's why He said not my will if this has to be done God, then You do it. I lay My will aside, and that is where all of us need to be. I tell you when we get in that place, there is no good thing that God is going to withhold from us because believe it or not, He is not withholding anything from us now.

It is not like God is up there grabbing all of your things that are supposed to be yours, saying. Un un. No, I am not going to let it get to her today. I am not going to let her have that today. He's not doing that because He's not that kind of God. He does not operate in the flesh like that.

What's happening is, we, being in the flesh, (carnal minded) are messing it up. You are asleep. You're missing all of the good things that God wants to share with you. But He can't share with you because you are in the flesh (carnal minded). So, verse 42 says:

"He went away again the second time, and

prayed, saying, O my Father, if this cup may not pass away from me, except I drink it, thy will be done" (Matthew 26:42 KJV).

Do it, God. Verse 43 says,

"And he came and found them asleep again: for their eyes were heavy (Matthew 26:43 KJV).

Verse 44

"And he left them, and went away again, and prayed the third time, saying the same words" (Matthew 26:44 KJV).

Oh, did you get that? So, if you have to keep on falling on your knees, if you've got to keep on, when I say keep on falling on your knees, it doesn't mean you gotta wait 'til you get to a place to fall on your knees. Really, what this represents if you have to keep humbling yourself, admitting to God, my flesh is weak. I want to do what You want me to do. But, I don't know how! Show me how to do what You want me to do. Show me, God, how to allow You to guide me in this path of life through this path where there is fullness of joy. God, show me how to do it in Jesus' name. And I tell you, you don't have to go and put a white hat on your head or dress up in white clothing, pretending that you are so holy.

You can just wear what you are wearing and just allow God to make you little by little into His image. "So God created human beings in his own image. In the image of God he created them; male and female he created them" (Genesis 1:27 NLT). God does not hit us on the head every time we make a mistake. That is where grace comes in at. But He wants us to be humble enough to say, God, I tried it, and I failed. It's ok to admit it because Jesus said the spirit is willing, but the flesh is weak. (The flesh represents the natural man.)

"Watch and pray, that ye enter not into temptation: the spirit indeed *is* willing, but the flesh *is* weak" (Matthew 26:41 KJV).

So, we've got to keep our flesh (the natural man) under subjection. You got to keep it in the presence of God. If you don't love God like you think God wants you to, just ask Him to teach you how to love Him. You know God knows how to do that and still give you a life? The love God is speaking of is to reverence Him—to fear Him. And the fear He is speaking of is to reverence Him.

"Reverence is defined as deep respect, or is a name given to a holy figure in a religious institution." An example of reverence is when you show deep and complete respect for the Bible as the Word of God. The respectful term used to address a priest is an example of reverence. verb 1. The definition of reverence is treating with great respect. When you treat a deity with great respect, this is an example of reverence.

See, some people don't want to do that; they want to keep one foot in the world, and one in the kingdom, which can't happen because you can't straddle the fence. He wants you hot or cold. He don't want you warm. He wants you hot. "I know thy works, that thou are neither cold nor hot: I would that thou wert cold or hot" (Revelations 3:15 KJV). So, if you can't do that, then you have to ask Him to help you to do that. And being the loving, gentle Father that He is, He is making you while you're sleeping. He is. He is changing your heart while you are at work. He's making you over while you are driving down the street in your car. And then the time will come when He will test, give you a test. And you know what? Unbeknownst to you, you will pass that test--and didn't even know you were prepared to take it. Somebody cuts over in the front of you; instead of you using obscene words or making bad gestures at them, you'll bless them because you are sanctified through Christ Jesus.

You *would*. I mean, where you were so quick tempered, you wouldn't be in agreement with anyone—always wanting to fight about everything. Now, you will find yourself being in agreement and at peace, thanking them for helping you. I mean, He will make you over, and you won't even know you are being made over. God will put people before you that you couldn't even stand to hear their names let alone look at them. You know Christians get like that. And you will find yourself wanting to give them a hug. Are you listening?™

You would have forgiven them and didn't even know you had. And all of a sudden, you realize you hold no animosity in your heart against that individual. God is making you over; HE is transforming your life. You refused to enter into a place where you knew you ought not to be. There was a time when you would just do it, and then have the nerve to try to explain it away.

But you get to a point in life when you will know: I'm not supposed to be here, and I am not going there. God is maturing you and all of a sudden, your eyes of understanding have been opened. God is transforming you from the old way into His way of doing things.

"And be not conformed to this world: but be ye transformed by the renewing of your mind, that ye may prove what *is* that good, and acceptable, and perfect, will

of God" (Romans 12:2 KJV). "And that ye put on the

new man, which after God is created in righteousness and

true holiness" (Ephesians 4:24 KJV). "And have put on

the new man, which is renewed in knowledge after the

image of him that created him:" (Colossians 3:10 KJV)

Chapter 9: TAKING A STAND

"Stand therefore, having your loins girt about with truth, and having on the breastplate of righteousness;" (Ephesians 6:14 KJV). The world will challenge you. The world (the people of the world) know how dedicated and passionate you are in your walk with Christ. They may not want to live it and want you to do as they do. But, they are not going to do what you ask them to do when it comes to the things of God. Are you listening? ™ So, it will get to the point when they try to make you feel like you ought to go to an ungodly, unrighteous, unChrist-like place with them, you'll take a stand and say No. I used to do stuff like that, but I'm born again now. The things I used to do for peace of mind, self-pleasure, to get ahead in life, I don't do those anymore. I don't go in those places anymore. I am a new creature in Christ Jesus.

17 Therefore if any man [be] in Christ, [he is] a new creature: old things are passed away; behold, all things are become new.

18 And all things [are] of God, who hath reconciled us to himself by Jesus Christ, and hath given to us the ministry of reconciliation;

19 To wit, that God was in Christ, reconciling the world unto himself, not imputing their trespasses unto them; and hath committed unto us the word of reconciliation.

20 Now then we are ambassadors for Christ, as though God did beseech [you] by us: we pray [you] in Christ's stead, be ye reconciled to God.

21 For he hath made him [to be] sin for us, who knew no sin; that we might be made the righteousness of God in him. (2 Corinthians 5:17-21 KJV)

Is anybody listening?™

I am going to give you one more scripture.

"Then cometh he to his disciples, and saith unto them, Sleep on now, and take your rest: behold, the hour is at hand, and the Son of man is betrayed into the hands of sinners" (Matthew 26:45 KJV).

And what He was saying is when I asked you to stay awake, the reason I brought you here to help pray me through, it's over now. He had to keep surrendering *His* will. And I am not going to say the disciples were out of the will of God because they weren't the ones that had to die. It was Jesus. He had to discipline *Himself* to the Will of God. In Luke Chapter 8 verse 21. They came to Jesus saying your mother and your brothers are out there calling for you. They want to see you; they want to talk to you.

Jesus was about the Father's business, so he said in verse 21:

"And he answered and said unto them, My mother and my brethren are these which hear the word of God, and do it"(Luke 8:21 KJV).

And so what He is saying here (and this is a h e a v y h a r d saying right here), but these are the words of Jesus. This is h e a v y. What He is saying here, He said, if you don't do the Will of The Father, you are not a brother. You're not a godly brother. Mistakes are going to be made, but *willfully* doing it your own way--I mean you know, you know the tree by the fruit it bears. If you keep on doing it your way, you're not a brother. You keep doing it your way, you're not a son. Because the Word of God says you have to believe on Jesus to become a son of God. John 1: 12 KJV: "But as many as received him, to them gave he power to become the sons of God, *even* to them that believe on his name:"

You are of your father that does what? Wrong, that is a liar. The Bible says he's the father of lies, talking about the devil. Philippians chapter 2, you can go there with me. Well, I know I have Philippians in my Bible, too. So, I found it. Chapter 2 verses 5-13. The key verse is 13.

"Let this mind be in you, which was also in Christ Jesus." (Philippians 2:5 KJV).

The reason the word "was" is here is because he is speaking of when Jesus was living as a man in the earth. Now, you hear this. Let this mind be in you, which is also in Christ Jesus. We just got through talking about Father, not my but Your will be done. That is what He said. Right? Let this mind be in you, which was also in Christ Jesus when He was in the earth as a man.

"Who, being in the form of God, thought it not robbery to be equal with God: But made himself of no reputation, and took upon him the form of a servant, and was made in the likeness of men:" (Philippians 2:6-7 KJV).

"...and took upon Him the form of a servant..." (See Philippians 2:6 KJV.)

"...and was made in the likeness of men...." (See Philippians 2:7 KJV)

"And being found in fashion as a man, he humbled himself, and became obedient unto death, even the death of the cross" (Philippians 2:8 KJV).

Now, look at that verse right there:

"Wherefore God also hath highly exalted him, and given him a name which is above every name:" (Philippians 2:9 KJV).

And let me tell you something, when we humble ourselves under the mighty hand of God that puts us in the will of God; there are pleasures in His right hand for ever more! Now, let us look at what happened when Jesus humbled Himself. By Him humbling Himself put Him in the will of God, and by Him(Christ) doing the will of God (through death, burial, and resurrection), Jesus Christ was exalted above every name in the Heavens, the Earth, and beneath the Earth! And GOD exalted Him above every name.

"Wherefore God also hath highly exalted him, and given him a name which is above every name:" (Philippians 2:9 KJV)

Hallelujah!! Oh Jesus! It is not too late to preach this. This will preach anywhere any day! But guess what?

There is something to gain--good things to gain when you humble yourself under the mighty will of God. He was exalted. So, if God exalted Him because He humbled Himself, HE will also exalt you--and me if we humble ourselves and hear what the Holy Spirit of God is saying to the body of Christ today. "Humble yourselves therefore under the mighty hand of God, that he may exalt you in due time:" (I Peter 5:6 KJV).

We will be in this world, but we will not be of this world. There will be suffering, and we don't take pleasure in suffering. But there will be suffering and lack and poverty and sickness and all that is around us. But we are only beholding those calamities with our eyes. Why? Because we are in His Will. There is something about being in the Will of God. It is just like being in His Presence. It is a covering, and you don't know peace and joy or contentment like you would know it if you were in His Will. God, what do You want me to do? I dare you to start praying that prayer! How do You want me to walk before You, God? It's not too late! If you think this is all to it right here, you have another thing coming. I am convinced that the strongholds that are on the body of Christ today is because there are so many people out of His will. I am going to do it the way I want to do it. You can't do it the way you want to do it and expect for the blessings of God to flow over it. He(Jesus)was exalted. See, I know you don't see that. I see it. He was exalted because He was in the will of God. Jesus took a stand and stood on the Plan of God.

"Wherefore God also hath highly exalted him, and given him a name which is above every name:" (Philippians 2:9 KJV).

"That at the name of Jesus every knee should bow, of things in heaven, and things in earth, and things under the earth;" (Philippians 2:10 KJV).

That's a good witness all because He gave His will to God.

"And that every tongue should confess that Jesus Christ is Lord, to the glory of God the Father. Wherefore, my beloved, as ye have always obeyed, not as in my presence only, but now much more in my absence, work out your own salvation with fear and trembling" (Philippians 2:11-12 KJV).

In other words, if you need to humble yourself, if you need to turn over your plate and fast, if you need to get alone with God, He said work this thing out. You don't have to do it in front of us. He said you work it out between you and God. "For it is God which worketh in you both to will and to do of his good pleasure" (Philippians 2:11-12 KJV).

Wait a minute. Who is it that does that? "…It is God, which workest in you, both to will and to do of His good pleasure. (See Philippians 2:11 KJV). And I told you, one of His good pleasures is to be in His will. At His right hand are pleasures for evermore.

You know, God is such a good God. And I know we don't always feel one hundred percent in our bodies, every day. If you do, God bless you. And even if you don't, God bless you so that that can happen. Amen. But we should keep ourselves in a position to be *always* on fire with the fire of The Holy Spirit. I'm telling you because we are *Christians*; we are *Christ followers*. We're made in His *image*.

Is anybody listening? ™ So, that alone ought to make us excited to want to do what God wants us to do.

There is no other message I could preach or teach now or any other time. There is no other message that I could preach but what God says. This may be stiff and sometimes boring to you. It might be heavy, but it's right. 'Cause HE is a *Father.* My Mama used to always say to me, Mama ain't going tell you nothing wrong, baby. Even if she was telling me something wrong, she thought it was right. Because she would never tell me anything to hurt me. Everything she said, it was to help me. Oh, Glory!

Point to yourself and say, *I am* a minister of the Gospel of Jesus Christ. Say: That's why God wants me to walk the Word--to be in His Will. Say: It is my duty to carry out the Word of God. My life is an example of God's Word. That's why I must humble myself to get in HIS presence, to get in HIS Will because if I don't do that, I cannot be like Jesus. My goal is to be *more* and *more* and *more* like Jesus. Look: reach out to someone and say these words: Will you pray for me? Ask them, Will you come into agreement with me? And I will be in agreement with you concerning whatever it may be. Say, Father, help me to be more like you in the name of Jesus. After you finish reading this book, I want you to go call a prayer partner, a neighbor, a friend, call someone you trust and ask if they would pray with you. Ask will you pray for me? Or you can call our church at 314-831-9525, and we will pray with you. Or go to our website: stclamin.org and leave your prayer request. Or you may write me Pastor Dorothy St. Clair, P. O. Box 3953, St. Louis, MO 63136, and we will get back with you.

I don't want you to feel like you have done something

wrong. This is all about growth. You have done nothing wrong. God wants us to know we can stay connected and grow in HIM. Now, I want you to remember who you have spoken with, who you have made this commitment with. Now, that commitment that you just made: are you serious? Will you pray for that person? Pray that they get into the Will of God.

There are times my husband and I are driving along the highway, and somebody's car has stopped on them, and they are out there fixing a tire on the highway. And I feel committed to say God--my husband will tell you I do it--I don't even know them by name. And right there I say to God, and I stretch my hand toward that person. I pray a prayer of safety for them that God would protect them on the highway and keep them safe as they take care of the need of their vehicle in Jesus' name. Thank you, Jesus.

CHAPTER 10: PRAYER OF SALVATION

I pray that you are feeling what I feel right now. I feel

the presence, the anointing of The Spirit of God. Maybe

you don't know this God I speak of today, this Jesus The

Christ--Hallelujah--that I speak of today. This Holy Spirit

I speak of in this book. Maybe you never had the

experience of asking HIM to come into your life. Oh,

people of God, this thing is real. God is not dead, He is

very much alive and so is Jesus for evermore. The Word

of God says in John 3:16: For God so loved the world

(unsaved people) that HE gave HIS only begotten Son to

die for us all that whosoever would believe on HIM would

not perish but have eternal life.

"For God so loved the world, that he gave his only begotten Son, that whosoever believeth in him should not perish, but have everlasting life" (John 3:16 KJV).

When HE said believe in Him, God is saying whosoever believes in Him(Christ) that Christ did die and that He was raised up again. He died for our sins to save us from a tormented hell to connect us back to God The Father again after the fall of Adam and Eve. The fall caused us all to die—caused separation between God and man. But Christ Jesus paid for that sin through His death by way of the cross and His resurrection and connected us back to God again, which gives us everlasting life. There is a Heaven to gain and a hell to shun. You may say, "What do I have to do to receive this salvation?" And I am going to say to you, just accept it; it is already given. All you have to do is receive it by asking Jesus to come into your life by repenting of your sins. Matthew 3:1-2 KJV: "In those days came John the Baptist, preaching in the wilderness of Judaea, And saying, Repent ye: for the kingdom of heaven is at hand." Revelation 3:20 says, Though I stand at the door and knock, if any man should open the door of his heart and let me come in, I will come in and sup with him and he with me. "Behold, I stand at the door, and knock: if any man hear my voice, and open the door, I will come in to him, and will sup with him, and he with me" (Revelation 3:20 KJV). Romans 10:9, If we confess with our mouth and believe in our heart that God has raised Jesus from the dead, we shall be saved.

Romans 10:9-13 KJV:

9 That if thou shalt confess with thy mouth the Lord Jesus, and shalt believe in thine heart that God hath raised

him from the dead, thou shalt be saved.

10 For with the heart man believeth unto righteousness; and with the mouth confession is made unto salvation.

11 For the scripture saith, Whosoever believeth on him shall not be ashamed.

12 For there is no difference between the Jew and the Greek: for the same Lord over all is rich unto all that call upon him.

13 For whosoever shall call upon the name of the Lord shall be saved.

The Bible also tells us that whosoever will, let him come. So, it doesn't matter what you have done or not done, Jesus The Christ is open to all. HE is open to all that will come.

Pray this prayer with me. Lord Jesus, I believe that you are the Son of God. The only one and true God. I believe that You did die for me. I believe that You are real. I repent of my sins, and I ask that You will come into my life. I receive salvation that You have already given to me. I receive it now. Make me one with You and The Father in Your name I pray. Amen.

Well, we did it again. This is all to it. Now, all you have to do is allow Him to live in you. Find yourself a good Bible-teaching church. Read the Bible. If you are in need of a Bible, just write to us, and we will send you one. Just know this, God so loved the world that HE gave HIS Son Jesus, and Jesus so loved us that He took on our sins and died for us. Thank you, Jesus. You are now a new creature in Christ Jesus. Amen! Hallelujah. Hallelujah. Hallelujah is the highest praise.

"Likewise, I say unto you, there is joy in the presence of the angels of God over one sinner that repenteth" (Luke 15:10 KJV).

"In the same way, there is joy in the presence of God's angels when even one sinner repents" (Luke 15:10 NLT).

God Bless you. We will see you in Volume 3.

About the Author

Pastor Dorothy St. Clair is a true Prophet/Pastor of God who operates in the Five-Fold Ministry (Ephesians 4:11 KJV "And he gave some, apostles; and some, prophets; and some, evangelists; and some, pastors and teachers;"). She has an in-season word in her mouth for the body of Christ. God uses her mightily in the area of prophecy. She has had three visitations from GOD. In the first visit, HE laid HIS hand upon her and anointed her for the work she is called to do. She is a Seasoned Prophet, Pastor, Revivalist, Teacher, Singer, Song Writer, Recording Artist, Conference Speaker,

Author, Publisher, and Radio, Television, and YouTube Minster…. She is founder and Senior Pastor along with her husband, Pastor Robert St. Clair. She has been active in ministry for more than 37 years. Pastor Dorothy is a devoted wife, mother, grandmother, woman of God, and spiritual mother to countless.

She is available upon request for guest speaking, revivals, and conference speaking.

In His Presence There is Fullness of Joy Vol. 1
is available at the following:

Print and ebook https://www.amazon.com

Ebook https://itunes.apple.com

Ebook https://play.google.com/store/books

Ebook https://www.kobo.com/us

Ebook https://www.barnesandnoble.com

Ebook https://www.ebooks2go.com

This book teaches one how to get in and stay
in the presence of God according to Psalms
16:11.

To contact the author write:

Pastor Dorothy St. Clair

P. O. Box 3953

St. Louis, MO 63136

Website: www.stclamin.org

Or call: (314) 831-9525

Pastor Dorothy St. Clair has prepared a table before you with the uncompromised Word of God and testimonies that will teach you how to walk in God's purpose and plan for your life. She encourages one to get in and stay in the presence of the LORD where there is fullness of joy.

Jesus *is* such a loving Savior. And what He wants us to know there is no temptation that is tempting you in any area that He has not already given you a way out of. Jesus is saying He has been there. He did not become Almighty until He had defeated death. So, everything that He had experienced at the point of His death and resurrection, He was experiencing it as we now experience it. But guess what? He was experiencing it in the will of God, which gave Him the ability to go through with it. He gave up His life--by the way--they *did not* take His life. "There hath no temptation taken you but such as is common to man: but God is faithful, who will not suffer you to be tempted above that ye are able; but will with the temptation also make a way to escape, that ye may be able to bear it" (1 Corinthians 10:13 KJV).

www.ingramcontent.com/pod-product-compliance
Lightning Source LLC
Chambersburg PA
CBHW071946100426
42736CB00042B/2143